WALT DISNEY WORLD®
RESORT

A MAGICAL
YEAR-BY-YEAR
JOURNEY

1998 EDITION

A Roundtable Press Book

New York

"The Twilight Zone®" is a registered trademark of CBS, Inc., and is used pursuant to a license from CBS, Inc.

GOOSEBUMPS and associated slogans are properties of Parachute Press, Inc. Based on the GOOSEBUMPS
book series by R. L. Stine published by Scholastic in the U.S. and other countries. © 1997 Parachute Press, Inc. All rights reserved.

Star Tours and Indiana Jones™ Epic Stunt Spectacular© Disney/Lucasfilm Ltd.
Star Wars and *Indiana Jones* are trademarks of Lucasfilm Ltd.

For Hyperion
Editor: Wendy Lefkon
Assistant Editor: Robin Friedman

For Roundtable Press, Inc.
Directors: Susan E. Meyer, Marsha Melnick
Design Concept: Michaelis/Carpelis Design
Text: Pam Brandon
Project Coordinator, Computer Production, Photo Editor, Designer: Steven Rosen

ISBN 0-7868-6386-2

FIRST EDITION
2 4 6 8 10 9 7 5 3 1

THE WORLD TO COME

DISNEY'S ANIMAL KINGDOM™ THEME PARK

THE OASIS

This welcoming entryway, a thick jungle of waterfalls, streams, grottoes, and meadows, and the animals that live there, sets the stage for Disney's Animal Kingdom™ Theme Park, a live-action adventure park based on mankind's endless fascination with animals. Home to more than a thousand creatures—real, imaginary, and extinct—Disney's Animal Kingdom Theme Park combines thrilling attractions, dramatic landscapes, and close encounters with exotic animals to create an unforgettable experience.

SAFARI VILLAGE

A blend of spicy, equatorial architecture from around the world, Safari Village is the crossroads of adventure and the hub through which guests pass to reach other lands. The colorful carvings, left and inset, are the work of artisans from the Indonesian island of Bali, a fusion of world folk-art culture including Colombian, Peruvian, African, and Polynesian forms. Towering 14 stories above Safari Village is The Tree of Life, the giant symbol of Disney's Animal Kingdom Theme Park™.

THE TREE OF LIFE

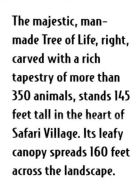

The majestic, man-made Tree of Life, right, carved with a rich tapestry of more than 350 animals, stands 145 feet tall in the heart of Safari Village. Its leafy canopy spreads 160 feet across the landscape.

AFRICA

Guests board Kilimanjaro Safaris, pictured in the rendering above, to explore more than 100 acres of savanna, forest, rivers, and rocky hills. Bouncing across the rugged terrain in an open-sided vehicle, guests experience close-up encounters with great herds of animals.

The adventure across the wilds of Africa begins in Harambe, a modern-day town on the edge of a wildlife reserve, above. The village is a mixture of traditional East African architecture mingled with simple, thatched structures. The photo at right shows Africa's realistic landscaping. There are 2.3 million plants—an astounding 260 species in all—at Disney's Animal Kingdom™ Theme Park.

The safari adventure takes guests across a rickety bridge, left, as they chase villainous poachers. Below, an actual view of the safari vehicles and Africa. Middle left, baobab trees, a symbol of the African savanna, beckon visitors.

Conservation Station, left, a center for conservation programs for Disney's Animal Kingdom™ Theme Park, provides a backstage look at the animal-care operations. Guests can meet animal experts and learn more about Disney's global commitment to wildlife.

AFRICA

Live, exotic animals, presented in true-life adventure stories of mystery, danger, and humor, help tell the dramatic story of wildlife in Africa today. The vast majority of animals will be born in zoological parks; others will be rescued from endangered habitats, or will be orphans that have been saved by wildlife officials.

DinoLand USA

A celebration of America's fascination with dinosaurs, DinoLand, USA, looks like a quirky roadside attraction. It features the Boneyard Playground, left, a rambling, open-air dig site filled with fossils for sliding, bouncing, and slithering. Guests encounter the triceratop, right, in the Countdown to Extinction thrill ride.

Dinosaurs of all shapes and sizes—from maternal plant-eaters to rampaging carnivores—inhabit the mist-shrouded forest in Countdown to Extinction (below). The thrill ride plunges guests back 65 million years to experience adventures in the Cretaceous era.

The Dino Institute, inset, is home to Countdown to Extinction, a wild journey that begins in Dr. Grant Seeker's quirky laboratory, where he has just perfected the time-rover vehicle. Guests enter a mysterious swamp, bumping, skidding, and diving along as Dr. Seeker guides the way; they come face to face with dinosaurs and cross the path of a giant asteroid that is hurtling toward Earth, bringing destruction in its wake.

THE WORLD
TO COME

EPCOT®

TEST TRACK

Buckle up for the longest, fastest ride in the history of the Walt Disney World® Resort— the new Test Track at Epcot. The attraction simulates an automotive proving ground and throws a dizzying array of maneuvers at guests.

DISNEY/MGM STUDIOS

FANTASMIC!

Fantasmic! is a nighttime spectacle that combines dancing waters, dazzling lasers, Disney villains, animation, and live performers. Inspired by the Disneyland show of the same name, shown here in photos top and left, Walt Disney World® Resort's Fantasmic! is scheduled to open at Disney-MGM Studios in 1998.

DisneyQuest™

DisneyQuest, "The Ultimate Interactive Adventure," debuts in 1998 at *Downtown Disney* West Side. Guests begin their journey at Ventureport, top right. Top left is the Score Zone, a superhero competition city; center, the Create Zone, a studio for artistic self-expression; bottom, the Explore Zone, a virtual adventureland; and right, the Replay Zone, a carnival on the moon with retro-futuristic rides and games.

Cirque du Soleil®

Magnificent Cirque du Soleil®—a striking mix of circus arts, special effects, and outrageous costumes—will premiere in 1998 at *Downtown Disney* West Side, with 72 avant-garde artists from all over the world. Renderings show exterior, top; the performance hall, left; and lobby, above.

DISNEY CRUISE LINES

Disney's first ship, *Disney Magic*, sets sail in early 1998, cruising from Port Canaveral to Nassau, Bahamas, and Castaway Cay, Disney's private island. The elaborately themed Animator's Palate dining room, above, begins with a completely black-and-white setting, then transforms into a full-color masterpiece, right.

1996-1997

MAGIC KINGDOM®PARK

MICKEY'S TOONTOWN FAIR (1996)

EVENTS
25th Anniversary Celebration (1996)

EPCOT®

FUTURE WORLD
Ellen's Energy Adventure (1996)

DISNEY/MGM STUDIOS

ATTRACTIONS
Disney's The Hunchback of Notre Dame,
a Musical Adventure (1996)
101 Dalmatians Special Effects
Tour (1996)
Goosebumps™ Horrorland (1997)

EVENTS
Disney's Hercules
"Zero to Hero"
Victory Parade
(1997)

BE OUR GUEST

Disney's Boardwalk Resort (1996)
Disney Institute (1996)
Disney's Coronado Springs Resort (1997)

THE REST OF THE WORLD

CITY OF CELEBRATION (1996)

**DISNEY'S WIDE WORLD OF SPORTS™
COMPLEX** (1996)

DOWNTOWN DISNEY WEST SIDE (1997)

FANTASIA GARDENS MINI-GOLF (1996)

**INDY 200 AT THE WALT DISNEY WORLD
SPEEDWAY** (1996)

MICKEY'S TOONTOWN FAIR

Mickey Mouse and his toon pals greet their fans in the newest Magic Kingdom land, set amidst candy-striped tents and a fanciful fairground, where kid-favorite attractions devoted to Mickey, Minnie, Donald Duck, and Goofy rekindle the old-fashioned excitement of a county fair.

Best of all, the Disney characters are there all day long, welcoming old friends and making new ones.

The Barnstormer, Goofy's Wiseacre Farm, opposite page, a kid-sized roller coaster, zips up and around a high-flying trackway before crashing through Goofy's barn at the climax of the topsy-turvy trip. Above, guests stroll by Mickey's Country House, with its cartoonish architecture. Top right, a youngster cools off in Miss Daisy, Donald's boat, which is a cross between a tugboat and a leaky ocean liner. Above, Donald Duck and friends salute from aboard, while splash-tastic adventures await. Left, a bronze statue honors Cornelius Coot, the founder of Duckburg, the town where Mickey's Toontown Fair takes place.

25th Anniversary Celebration

The Magic Kingdom® Park is the center of the biggest celebration in the history of the Walt Disney World® Resort. Festivities include an all-new Remember the Magic Parade, which salutes returning guests and the world's largest birthday cake: Cinderella Castle transformed with bright pink icing, giant lollipops, gumdrops, and 26 towering candles (one to grow on).

EPCOT ®

ELLEN'S ENERGY ADVENTURE

DID YOU KNOW?

The roof of the Universe of Energy is covered with two acres of photovoltaic cells, which convert sunlight directly into electrical energy, providing 15 percent of the power required to run the attraction inside.

Ellen DeGeneres and Bill Nye, right, bring comedy to Epcot guests in the redesigned Universe of Energy pavilion, renovated in 1996. The new attraction takes visitors on a humorous journey back to the beginning of time to learn about energy. Life-size dinosaurs, above, make this a favorite attraction for youngsters.

1996
1997

Disney's The Hunchback of Notre Dame, A Musical Adventure

An elaborate, Broadway-style production tells the story of the Notre Dame bell ringer Quasimodo and the gypsy Esmeralda, with a cast of twenty-one and the music of Alan Menken and Stephen Schwartz. Elaborate costumes and sets and a cast of miniature medieval puppets re-create 15th-century Paris.

101 Dalmatians Special Effects Tour

This attraction features dazzling special effects, authentic costumes, and sets from the zany live-action film. Guests see Cruella's original outfits, above, and her $500,000 car, the Panther DeVil, right, made exclusively for the movie.

DISNEY'S HERCULES "ZERO TO HERO" VICTORY PARADE

Hercules gets his very own homecoming parade every day at the Disney/MGM Studios, transporting guests back to ancient Greece to witness a wacky salute to the Big Olive's "greatest hero of all time." Even the wicked Hades himself, top right, gets a starring role.

1996
1997

Goosebumps™ Horrorland

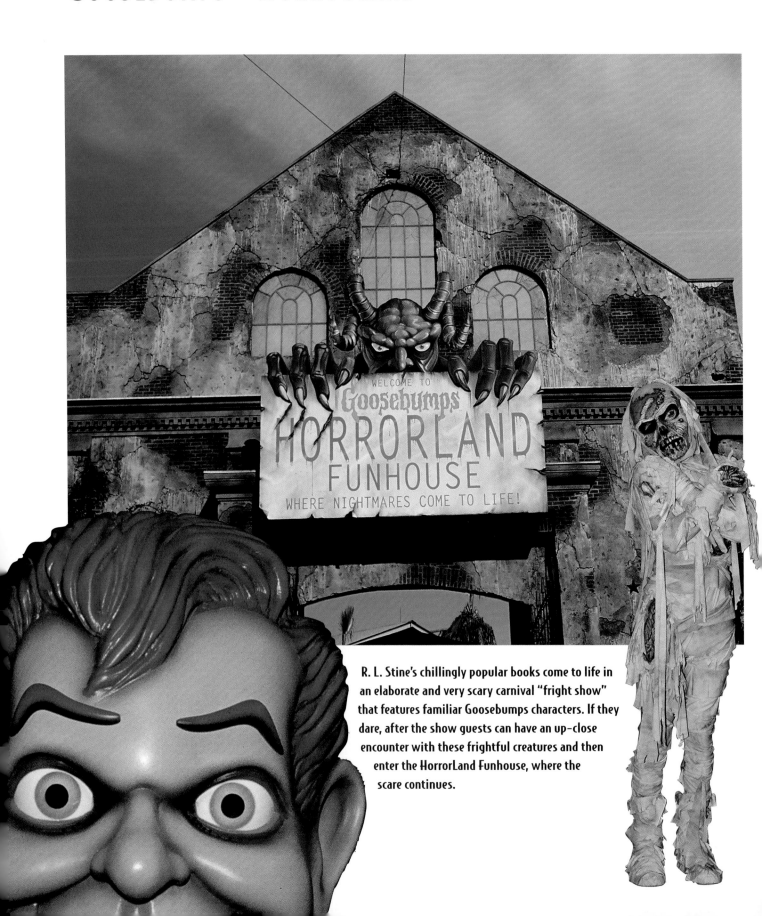

R. L. Stine's chillingly popular books come to life in an elaborate and very scary carnival "fright show" that features familiar Goosebumps characters. If they dare, after the show guests can have an up-close encounter with these frightful creatures and then enter the HorrorLand Funhouse, where the scare continues.

BE OUR GUEST

DISNEY'S BOARDWALK RESORT

Capturing the charm and flavor of the 1930s mid-Atlantic coast, this resort features an exciting entertainment district that includes restaurants, shopping, and nightclubs, like Jellyrolls, above, where you can sing along with dueling pianos. An eclectic mix of stripes and florals, overstuffed sofas, and giant palms create a relaxed elegance in the resort lobby, below.

1996
1997

DISNEY INSTITUTE

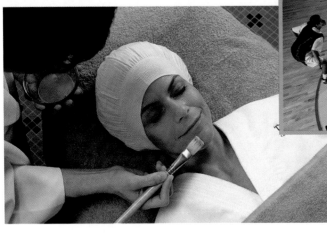

Every day is different at The Disney Institute, an innovative resort and spa located near the Walt Disney World® Resort theme parks, where guests get to custom design their own vacations. Appealing to a sense of discovery, exploration, and wonder, there are dozens of hands-on programs to choose from, like gardening, top right, or computer animation, right, all taught by entertaining experts with a Disney point of view. The lakeside enclave, top, is on the beautiful Lake Buena Vista Golf Course. Personalized therapies are offered at the Spa at the Disney Institute, above, and there are plenty of sports activities in the adjacent Sports and Fitness Center, center photo.

DISNEY'S CORONADO SPRINGS RESORT

With playful pastels and fancy mosaic accents re-creating the American Southwest and Mexico, Disney's newest resort takes guests back to the days of explorer Francisco de Coronado and his search for the fabled lost city of Cibola.

CITY OF CELEBRATION

After more than a decade of planning, Celebration, a new town in Osceola County designed by The Celebration Company, a subsidiary of the Walt Disney Company, welcomed its first residents. Noted architects, such as Michael Graves, Robert A. M. Stern, and Philip Johnson, designed the downtown buildings, like the Preview Center tower, top left, and the waterfront buildings, left. Apartments, above, are a short stroll to downtown.

Disney's Wide World of Sports™ Complex

Guests can catch some of the country's greatest professional and amateur athletes at the new sports complex in a design that recalls all-American ballparks from a century ago, above. An exhibition game between the Atlanta Braves and the Cincinnati Reds, left. The Braves begin spring training here in 1998.

Downtown Disney West Side

A striking new skyline defines this new high-energy showplace of nightclubs, spectacular theaters, celebrity restaurants, and shopping adventures. Inset above, the Wolfgang Puck® Cafe; below left, the distinctive neon of Magnetron and AMC® Pleasure Island 24 Theatres Complex; below right, on stage at the House of Blues™.

Fantasia Gardens Mini-Golf

Disney's classic film *Fantasia* is the inspiration for this 18-hole miniature golf course, which includes dancing fountains and cleverly themed hazards based on the movie.

Indy 200 at the Walt Disney World Speedway

The initial running gained a place in motorsports history as the inaugural event of the Indy Racing League. The annual run is one of a series of races "on the road" to the famed Indianapolis 500.

1996
1997

1995

 MAGIC KINGDOM® PARK

NEW TOMORROWLAND
    THE EXTRATERRORESTRIAL
     ALIEN ENCOUNTER
    ASTRO ORBITER
    THE TIMEKEEPER
    GALAXY PALACE THEATER

 EPCOT®

FUTURE WORLD
    GLOBAL NEIGHBORHOOD

 **DISNEY/MGM STUDIOS**

EVENTS
    DISNEY'S TOY STORY PARADE
    SPECTACLE OF LIGHTS

 **THE REST OF THE WORLD**

DISNEY'S WEDDING PAVILION

DINING AROUND THE WORLD

DISNEY'S BLIZZARD BEACH

NEW TOMORROWLAND

The future that never was…is here. New Tomorrowland borrows from the fantasy of science fiction writers and moviemakers of the '20s and '30s to create a fantasy future with planet-hopping aliens, time-machine travel, and a Flash Gordon–inspired neighborhood with rich, bold colors and miles of neon. The overall effect is a friendly intergalactic city, with some of the newest Magic Kingdom attractions, plus revised versions of longtime favorites.

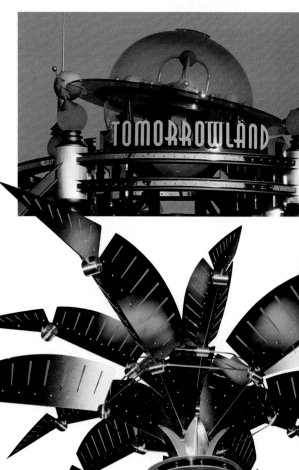

Walt Disney Imagineers designed the stylish Avenue of the Planets, above, as the distinctive entryway to New Tomorrowland. This canyon of glistening metal trimmed in light, has the rings of the Astro Orbiter flashing celestial colors as a beacon at the end of the street. The artistic version of "the future that never was" pays homage to early-19th-century visionaries like Jules Verne, but lightens up with characters like Sunny Eclipse, left, the hilarious lounge singer who performs in Cosmic Ray's Starlight Café.

1995

The ExtraTERRORestrial Alien Encounter

Guests buckle up for a demonstration of a new teleportation system in the ExtraTERRORestrial Alien Encounter, but an attempt to transport a friendly creature from another planet to Earth fails, and the catastrophic results are a close encounter with a frightening alien creature, above. Right, guests get their first glimpse of the gruesome creature seconds before it manages to escape into the theater.

Astro Orbiter

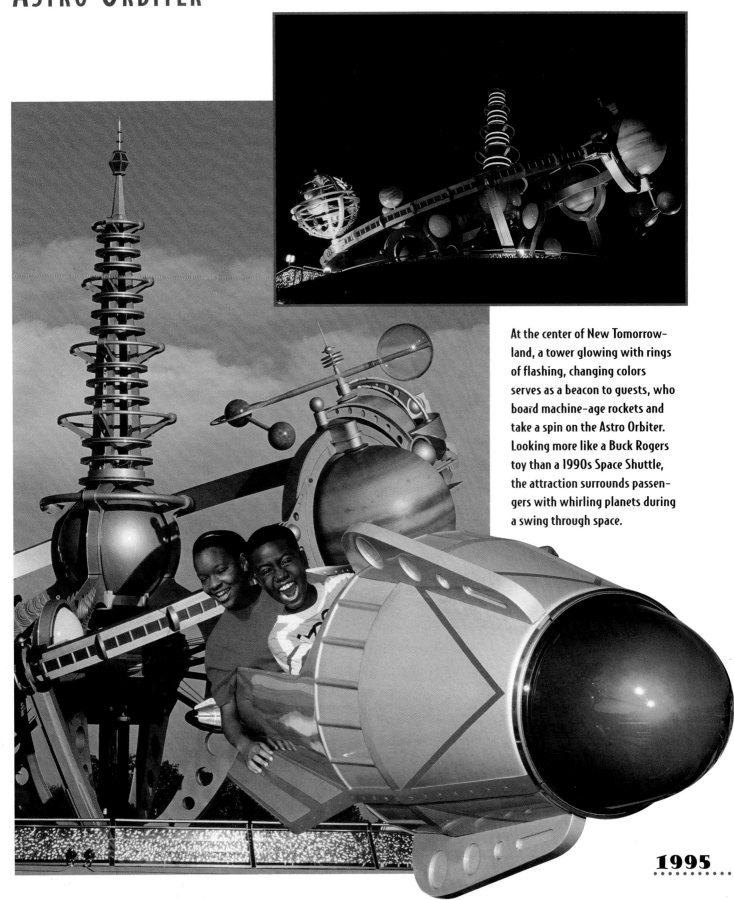

At the center of New Tomorrow-land, a tower glowing with rings of flashing, changing colors serves as a beacon to guests, who board machine-age rockets and take a spin on the Astro Orbiter. Looking more like a Buck Rogers toy than a 1990s Space Shuttle, the attraction surrounds passengers with whirling planets during a swing through space.

1995

THE TIMEKEEPER

Like a hovering spaceship, the intriguing exterior of The Timekeeper beckons, above. Disney combines Circle-Vision 360 technology with Audio-Animatronics and special effects to create a time-travel adventure. Left, a pair of robots called Timekeeper and 9-Eye (so named because she has nine cameras that serve as eyes) are the hosts of this journey.

Galaxy Palace Theater

Zany creatures from every corner of the cosmos perform in Galaxy Search, an intergalactic talent competition on the Galaxy Palace Theater's outdoor stage, right. Mickey Mouse hosts this far-out contest, starring King, below right, a 3-eyed-lizard Elvis impersonator from planet Elvis Centauri, decked out in rhinestone shades, holographic jewels, and, of course, sideburns.

1995

EPCOT®

GLOBAL NEIGHBORHOOD

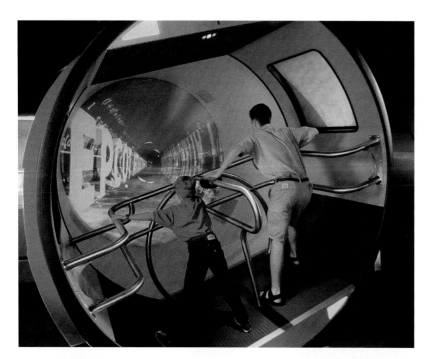

This interactive computer-video wonderland at the finale of Spaceship Earth includes a motion-simulator ride through the fibers and airwaves of a worldwide information network, left, as well as other hands-on activities that showcase 21st-century technology.

DID YOU KNOW?

Michelle Davi of Port Jefferson Station, N.Y., is honored as the 500-millionth guest to visit a Walt Disney World® Resort theme park, along with husband, John, daughter, Jenna, and son, John.

DISNEY'S TOY STORY PARADE

Buzz Lightyear, Woody, and all the toys from Disney's hit animated film *Toy Story* starred in their very own parade at the Disney/MGM Studios. The Green Army Men, inset, were a favorite of guests.

1995

SPECTACLE OF LIGHTS

Little Rock, Arkansas, businessman Jennings Osborne's brilliant display of holiday cheer—more than 2 million twinkling lights—cover the Disney/MGM Studios Residential Street and New York Street backlot with a dazzling blanket of Christmas color, including a 760-foot stretch of lights, above. The first display featured a seven-story tree, 60 flying angels, and two 20-foot-tall carousels. Osborne, who gained worldwide attention for the giant light display he created for his daughter in 1986, moved the lights from his home in Little Rock to Walt Disney World® Resort.

DISNEY'S WEDDING PAVILION

Fairy tales, like dreams, come true, with Cinderella's glass coach drawn by six white ponies waiting to whisk couples to Disney's Wedding Pavilion, above. Built on a private island surrounded by Seven Seas Lagoon, below, the elegant, glass-enclosed pavilion offers a picturesque backdrop of Cinderella Castle, perfectly framed in a window behind the altar.

1995

DINING AROUND THE WORLD

There's a dramatic new chapter in Walt Disney World dining: talented chefs are turning out delicious fare—and redefining the Vacation Kingdom as a sophisticated culinary destination. With vacationers seeking everything from a scrumptious burger to a magnificent gourmet meal, even the long-time theme park favorites have new menus emphasizing creativity and freshness. Bon appetit!

Kids of all ages adore Mickey Mouse, and one of the best places to find the Big Cheese is Chef Mickey's, above and left, at Disney's Contemporary Resort. A kid-friendly buffet and a guaranteed stop at the table by the Disney characters make this a favorite dining spot.

High atop Disney's Contemporary Resort is the California Grill, right, where Chef Clifford Pleau, far right, is setting new standards with his award-winning cuisine. High-energy chefs in the exhibition kitchen give diners a dazzling show, competing with a panoramic view of the Magic Kingdom® Park. The extraordinary wine list and impeccable wait staff are the icing on the cake.

Chef John State, below, offers innovative cuisine in the dreamy Flying Fish Café on Disney's BoardWalk, left. Lively Spoodles, bottom left, brings a taste of the Mediterranean to the BoardWalk. Chef Scott Hunnel, middle right, invites guests into his kitchen at the Chef's Table in Victoria & Albert's at Disney's Grand Floridian Beach Resort & Spa, bottom right.

1995

DISNEY'S BLIZZARD BEACH

A ski resort in the midst of a tropical lagoon? Disney storytellers came up with a whopper this time: a freak winter storm dropped a mountain of snow on the western side of Disney property, and a quick-thinking entrepreneur built Florida's first ski resort. But temperatures soared and the snow melted, leaving liquid slopes. Voilà! A water park was created.

Whether bobsledding or bouncing over and around moguls, guests get all the thrills of a northern ski resort—even a chair lift to carry daredevils to Summit Plummet, the world's tallest, fastest speed slide, where riders reach speeds of up to 55 miles per hour as they plunge straight down to a splash landing.

Mt. Gushmore tops out at 90 feet, with a spectacular view of all the action below.

1995

1994

 ## MAGIC KINGDOM® PARK

FANTASYLAND
THE LEGEND OF THE LION KING
SNOW WHITE'S ADVENTURES
(RENOVATION)

EVENTS
MICKEY MANIA PARADE

 ## EPCOT®

FUTURE WORLD
HONEY, I SHRUNK THE AUDIENCE
INNOVENTIONS
THE LAND
(RENOVATION)

EVENTS
EPCOT INTERNATIONAL FLOWER & GARDEN
FESTIVAL

 ## DISNEY/MGM STUDIOS

ATTRACTIONS
THE TWILIGHT ZONE TOWER OF TERROR
SUNSET BOULEVARD

 ## BE OUR GUEST

DISNEY'S WILDERNESS LODGE
DISNEY'S ALL-STAR SPORTS & MUSIC
RESORTS

 ## THE REST OF THE WORLD

PLEASURE ISLAND
PLANET HOLLYWOOD

WALT DISNEY WORLD MARATHON

WALK AROUND THE WORLD

CHRISTMAS AROUND THE WORLD

THE LEGEND OF THE LION KING

Favorite characters from Disney's hit animated film *The Lion King* come to life in Fantasyland's imaginative Legend of the Lion King stage show, combining puppetry, special effects, and music. Top left, wise Rafiki is the narrator; top right, a young Simba with Timon; and left, the lively cast of jungle characters on the elaborate set.

SNOW WHITE'S ADVENTURES (RENOVATION)

Known as Snow White's Scary Adventures since 1971, the attraction was revised to make it more enjoyable for young guests and now features brighter colors and a lighter style closer to the original Walt Disney movie classic, with artwork based on scenes from the film.

1994

MICKEY MANIA PARADE

"Rock the House with the Mouse" was the theme song for this madcap parade of everything Mickey that rolled down Main Street U.S.A. Every detail was "Mickeyized," with mouse-eared polka dots covering the floats, balloons, and costumes of dancers, singers, stilt walkers, roller bladers, bikers, skateboards, musicians, and Disney characters. The parade mirrored the worldwide phenomenon of Mickey images on fashions, clocks and watches, toys, and more in nearly every country of the world.

EPCOT ®

HONEY, I SHRUNK THE AUDIENCE

The sensation of shrinking to a teeny-tiny size is just one of the believ-able effects inthe Imagination pavilion's *Honey, I Shrunk the Audience*, inspired by the hilarious hit films *Honey, I Shrunk the Kids* and *Honey, I Blew Up the Baby*, and featuring Eric Idle and Marcia Strassman. 3-D glasses put guests smack in the middle of the mayhem, with incredible "4-D" effects that leave everyone squealing and squirming in their seats.

1994

INNOVENTIONS

At the launch of Innoventions in 1994, Disney CEO Michael Eisner said, "People need a place to experience the near future, a permanent world's fair, where they can test and try the products that are changing their world." Designed to turn "future shock" into "future fascination," Innoventions surrounds guests with exciting shows, demonstrations, and hands-on displays. Disney's talent for storytelling is combined with the advanced technologies of the world's best companies to showcase products that are quickly changing the way we live. From virtual reality to electronic shopping, it's a fun, friendly way to ease into the information revolution.

There are gadgets and gizmos galore: a souped-up stereo blasts from under the hood of a fancy pickup, top left, one of the original Innoventions exhibits. The 50,000-square-foot playground lets guests indulge their interest in technology without intimidation, left. Above top, a nighttime view of Innoventions Plaza, with glowing billboards and bright fiber optics in the sidewalk. Guests get a firsthand experience with virtual reality, above, while stand-up comedian Alec Tronic, right, demonstrates the amazing Audio-Animatronic technology used in many Disney attractions.

THE LAND (RENOVATION)

The six-acre Land pavilion gets a light, airy new look, with pastels replacing the original earth tones, and more colorful, hot-air balloons floating to the skylights. Sunshine Season Food Fair, above, brings the outdoors indoors, with splashing fountains and informal seating under oversized patio umbrellas. Animation and live footage tell a tale of environmental dangers in *Circle of Life*, above right, in the pavilion's Harvest Theater.

Parodies of classic rock 'n' roll songs deliver the message of good nutrition in Food Rocks, with singing kitchen utensils, left, and a "heavy metal" group, below.

EPCOT® International Flower & Garden Festival

Each spring, Disney gardening experts work to "paint" Future World and World Showcase with more than 30 million blooms, creating a fragrant, monthlong extravanganza of flowers. Magnificent topiary, like *Fantasia,* left, and *Beauty and the Beast,* inset, are showcased throughout the park, with gardening workshops, behind-the-scenes tours, and entertainment featured.

1994

The TWILIGHT ZONE TOWER of TERROR®

The plummet is 13 stories and the fright is unforgettable, with not one but two terrifying drops in pitch darkness down an elevator shaft. It's "The Twilight Zone Tower of Terror," and the deserted Hollywood Tower Hotel tells the secret of what happened one stormy night when five guests disappeared from the hotel elevator. Inspired by *The Twilight Zone* TV series, the old hotel is full of strange sights and sounds—but none more frightening than the view when the doors open at 13 stories just before the dreaded drop.

An early model, left, shows the eerie exterior of the thrill ride, a relic of Hollywood's Golden Age. The extravagantly decorated lobby of the hotel, above top, features antiques circa 1939, when, as legend goes, a violent storm struck the building and an entire guest wing disappeared along with an elevator carrying five people. Riders navigate spooky hallways and the dusty boiler room before boarding freight elevators for a trip to the fifth dimension, culminating in more than one hair-raising plunge, above.

At 199 feet, the Hollywood Tower Hotel is the tallest Walt Disney World® Resort attraction, featuring a thrilling drop from 13 stories.

1994

SUNSET BOULEVARD

Sunset Boulevard pays tribute to Hollywood's theater district in all its glory, with color-drenched facades derived from famous landmarks like the Beverly Wilshire Theater and Carthay Circle Theater, where *Snow White and the Seven Dwarfs* had its premiere in 1937.

DISNEY'S WILDERNESS LODGE

Tons of granite flagstone and hundreds of giant lodgepole pines from the West were used to create this grand hideaway, inspired by rustic, century-old national park lodges. The sun-drenched atrium, below, is graced by massive chandeliers with torch-cut scenes of Indians and buffalo topped with glowing teepees, and two 55-foot hand-carved totem poles, detail at left. The dramatic exterior, bottom left, includes wooden boardwalks and an "Old Faithful"–style geyser that erupts up to 100 feet in the air at regular intervals.

1994

DISNEY'S ALL-STAR SPORTS & MUSIC RESORTS

Gigantic football helmets, tennis rackets, cowboy boots, and maracas are some of the larger-than-life icons at these two resorts, where theme architecture and landscaping all work together to make a fantastic setting.

Planet Hollywood™

There's more star power at Pleasure Island, site of this eatery, owned by Arnold Schwarzenegger, Bruce Willis, Demi Moore, and other actors. World headquarters for the chain, this three-level restaurant, in the shape of a giant globe, is packed with TV and film memorabilia.

1994

WALT DISNEY WORLD MARATHON

Thousands of runners from around the world compete in Disney's annual marathon, often dubbed the most magical 26.2 miles in the world for the combination of theme park scenery and lively entertainment all along the course. The event starts predawn at Epcot®, winds its way through the Magic Kingdom® Park as the sun rises, left, then on to the Disney/MGM Studios. At the finish line, Mickey Mouse greets a weary but jubilant runner, above.

WALK AROUND THE WORLD

CAL GROGAN
LOVE IS A SONG
THAT NEVER ENDS

WAREHAM, MA
C08 ✦ 189
C08 ✦ 191
95

Thousands of bricks, all personalized in some way for Disney guests, have begun to encircle the Seven Seas Lagoon to create the Walk Around the World. The walk eventually will comprise more than 400,000 bricks in shades of red, brown, and charcoal, stretching more than three miles around the lagoon. The 10-inch hexagonal paving bricks feature a silhouette of Mickey Mouse or a specialized wedding bell, anniversary ring, or friendship-romance logo plus engraving.

1994

CHRISTMAS AROUND THE WORLD

Tall fir trees covered with colorful lights… carolers harmonizing the songs of the season …old-fashioned holiday decorations everywhere…An idyllic picture of the holidays comes to life at Walt Disney World® Resort, with special holiday festivities in all three theme parks and beyond. From the very first holiday season in 1971, Disney has created a special winter getaway, adding new surprises every year. Now more than 14 miles of garland are strung throughout the resort, and there are 400 Christmas trees, ranging from the tabletop variety to those towering more than 70 feet.

Opposite page top, the Singing Christmas Tree in the Magic Kingdom® Park, before the annual Candle-light Processional moved to Epcot® in 1994. The Magic Kingdom Park in all its holiday splendor, opposite page. Above, a canopy of 30,000 lights, one of the newest holiday additions at Epcot. Far left, the Earffel Tower at the Disney/MGM Studios gets a Christmas cap—size 342 3/8. Left top, tuba players get in the holiday spirit, and, left, the Disney/MGM Studios' Christmas tree.

1994

1990-1993

MAGIC KINGDOM® PARK

FRONTIERLAND
Splash Mountain (1992)

LIBERTY SQUARE
Hall of Presidents (1993)
(renovation)

TOMMOROWLAND
Carousel of Progress (1993)
(renovation)

EVENTS
The Sword in the Stone (1993)
World Wide Kids Day (1993)
20th Anniversary Surprise
Celebration (1991)
Spectromagic Parade (1991)

DISNEY/MGM STUDIOS

ATTRACTIONS
Honey I Shrunk the Kids Movie Set
Adventure (1990)
Star Tours (1990)
Sci-Fi Dine-In Theater (1991)
Jim Henson's MuppetVision 3D (1991)
Voyage of the Little Mermaid (1992)
"Beauty and the Beast"–Live on
Stage (1991)

EVENTS
Aladdin's Royal Caravan Parade (1992)
Sorcery in the Sky (1990)
Macy's Balloons (1992)

BE OUR GUEST

Disney's Old Key West Resort (1992)
Walt Disney World Swan® and
Dolphin (1990)
Disney's Port Orleans Resort (1991)
Disney's Dixie Landings Resort (1992)
Disney's Yacht and Beach
Club Resorts (1990)

THE REST OF THE WORLD

PLEASURE ISLAND
Pleasure Island Jazz Company (1993)

GOLF AROUND THE WORLD

SPLASH MOUNTAIN

This action-packed journey takes riders in flume logs through magnificent scenes inspired by Walt Disney's 1946 film, *Song of the South*, starring a happy-go-lucky Brer Rabbit and his antagonists, Brer Fox and Brer Bear. The rollicking adventure culminates when Brer Rabbit, along with Splash Mountain guests, plunge over the top of a steep spillway, whizzing from the mountaintop to a splashdown five stories below—faster than any other Magic Kingdom attraction. The rousing finale, left, features 12 animated characters singing "Zip-A-Dee-Doo-Dah" as the showboat rocks in time to the music.

1990
1993

HALL OF PRESIDENTS/CAROUSEL OF PROGRESS (RENOVATIONS)

U.S. President Bill Clinton gets a speaking role in the Hall of Presidents, with all 42 chief executives on stage, above. New narration for the attraction is the lilting voice of poet Maya Angelou. At right, the popular Carousel of Progress gets an updated script and a return to the original theme song, "There's a Great Big Beautiful Tomorrow."

The Sword in the Stone

Worldwide Kids Day

Merlin works his magic, and a youngster is able to pull the sword from the stone in a daily ceremony in Fantasyland, above. In 1993, 6,500 disadvantaged children from around the world came to Walt Disney World® Resort.

20th Anniversary Surprise Celebration

This carnival of larger-than-life Disney characters brought a Mardi Gras ambience to Main Street U.S.A. Mickey, Minnie, Pluto, Donald, and Goofy appeared as gigantic, colorful cold-air balloons that towered nearly 40 feet in the air. Floats and a cast of more than 100 performers completed the daily caravan. Cinderella Castle hot-air balloons flew in cities across the U.S. as part of the 20th gala.

Spectromagic Parade

Favorite Disney characters light up Main Street U.S.A., in the grand nighttime spectacle.

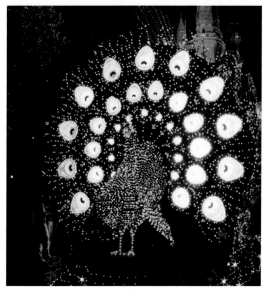

More than 600,000 miniature lights move in perfect concert with sound effects and music in this high-tech extravaganza. Mickey Mouse, far left, plays the role of a magician, capable of altering colors, brilliance, and lighting effects.

1990
1993

DISNEY/MGM STUDIOS

HONEY, I SHRUNK THE KIDS MOVIE SET ADVENTURE

Stalks of grass are 30 feet high, cereal is the size of truck tires, and ants are big enough to ride in this giant-size wonderland, inspired by Disney's blockbuster, *Honey, I Shrunk the Kids.* Guests are in for a hilarious adventure as they discover what it's like to be miniaturized in this oversized backyard full of tunnels, slides, rope ladders, and oversized props.

STAR TOURS

It's an uproarious flight to the moon of Endor in this wild galactic journey. The adventure begins on a woodland path beneath the village of the Ewoks, left, with a battle-disabled Imperial walker looking down on the Ewoks' treetop homes. Droids, below, work for a galactic travel agency servicing the Star Tours fleet of spacecraft. Bottom right, passengers board for the spine-tingling flight to Endor, with flight-simulator technology and a thrill-a-second motion picture creating a *Star Wars* experience. Endor Vendors, the shop outside Star Tours, offers intergalactic souvenirs.

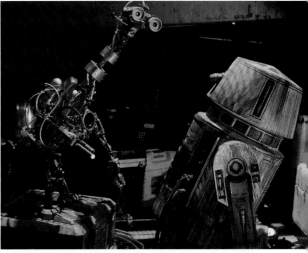

1990
1993

Sci-Fi Dine-In Theater

This unique restaurant is a nostalgic re-creation of a drive-in theater with flashy, 1950s-era convertibles as tables and fiber-optic stars twinkling overhead. Campy sci-fi trailers and cartoons play nonstop on the giant movie screen, with free popcorn for an appetizer.

JIM HENSON'S MUPPETVISION 3D

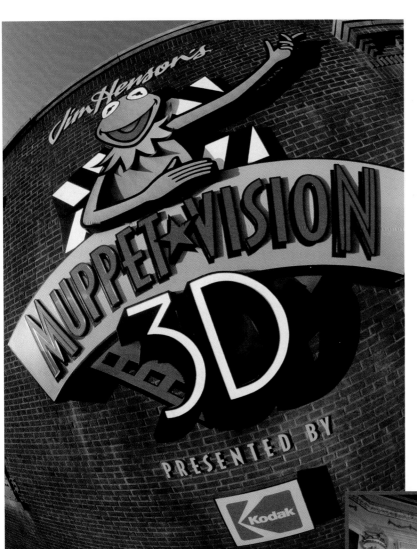

The audience puts on 3-D glasses for this uproarious "4-D" attraction—"4-D" because of the sensational in-theater effects. The Muppet Lab "scientists" cook up convincing 3-D tricks, like the pie-throwing sequence, right, with Kermit the Frog and Fozzie Bear. All the favorite Muppet characters make an appearance; some even show up live in the theater during the sensational show.

1990
1993

VOYAGE OF THE LITTLE MERMAID

A live musical adapted from the animated classic tells the enchanting tale of Ariel and Prince Eric, right, with friends Sebastian and Flounder. Ursula, the evil sea witch, above, is back to steal Ariel's voice.

ALADDIN'S ROYAL CARAVAN PARADE

This colorful procession was inspired by the hit movie starring a big blue genie and a young Aladdin, along with his frisky sidekick monkey, Abu, and beautiful Princess Jasmine. A pair of golden camels, left, surprised spectators by turning their heads and spitting cold water as they were pulled through the streets. Even Aladdin's old nemesis, Jafar, was part of the parade.

SORCERY IN THE SKY

Dramatic pyrotechnics celebrate the landmark Disney film *Fantasia* by animating the sky in colors that dance to newly recorded music from the classic, plus a host of other memorable movies. Mickey Mouse makes a surprise appearance in the finale, in the form of a 55-foot-high inflatable figure atop a replica of the Chinese Theatre.

MACY'S BALLOONS

It may look like Manhattan, but it's the Disney/MGM Studios, where giant Goofy and Betty Boop inflatables, originals from Macy's Thanksgiving Day parade, floated above the backlot facades on New York Street—a once-in-a-lifetime re-creation of the famous parade scene.

"Beauty and the Beast"—Live on Stage

The mesmerizing love story of Belle and the Beast comes to life in this musical extravaganza at Theatre of the Stars, starring all of the film's endearing characters in a classic fairy tale filled with action, humor, and romance.

**1990
1993**

BE OUR GUEST

DISNEY'S OLD KEY WEST RESORT

Disney Vacation Club's flagship resort features luxury island homes in a Key West setting and a festive boardwalk, right, with themed restaurants, swimming pools, tennis courts, and other recreation. The lighthouse, above, is really a deluxe sauna.

WALT DISNEY WORLD SWAN AND DOLPHIN

Giant, graceful dolphins and swans, left and bottom, take Disney's "entertainment architecture" to new heights, perched high atop these two distinctive hotels. Designed by noted architect Michael Graves, the hotels were the beginning of a new era in Disney design.

Dazzling turquoise and coral interiors of both hotels include more dolphins and swans, parrots, toucans and other creatures throughout, with tenting in the large interior spaces of the Dolphin, above, to resemble a cabana.

1990
1993

DISNEY'S PORT ORLEANS RESORT

Ornate buildings re-create the charm of the French Quarter in this resort, featuring a pool area highlighted by a colorful sea serpent slide that emerges from the water in a blaze of purple and turquoise, left. Below, the picturesque waterway connects Disney's Port Orleans resort to the shops and showplaces of the Downtown Disney area.

DISNEY'S DIXIE LANDINGS RESORT

Disney's Dixie Landings resort depicts the lifestyle of the great Old South with stately mansions and rustic bayou dwellings amid trees and flowers. The man-made Sassagoula River winds through the heart of the resort. At Dixie Levee, above left, guests can board a boat or rent bikes to explore shady paths along the river.

1990
1993

DISNEY'S YACHT AND BEACH CLUB RESORTS

This New England–style resort evokes images of seashore hotels of the late 1800s with a whimsical lighthouse, right, that welcomes guests back from Walt Disney World® Resort attractions. Just west of EPCOT®, Spaceship Earth peeks over the horizon, below. The resort's adjacent convention center is elegantly decorated to look like a grand, turn-of-the century meeting hall with spacious rooms, like the one below right.

PLEASURE ISLAND JAZZ COMPANY

Smooth jazz is at home on Pleasure Island in this sophisticated setting for concerts by an eclectic variety of nationally recognized musicians. Opened in 1993 as jazz returned to popularity, the mood is contemporary '90s mainstream, featuring recording artists and stars from Memphis and Chicago to New Orleans and San Francisco. The acoustically perfect performance room gives even those in the back of the house the feeling of being right on stage.

GOLF AROUND THE WORLD

With the addition of Disney's Osprey Ridge and Disney's Eagle Pines courses in 1992, Walt Disney World® Resort now features 99 holes, making it one of the largest golf resorts in the country. Disney's Bonnet Creek Golf Clubhouse, above, serves both new courses.

1990
1993

1989

MAGIC KINGDOM® PARK

TOMORROWLAND
Take Flight

EVENTS
Disney Character Hit Parade

EPCOT®

FUTURE WORLD
Wonders of Life

DISNEY/MGM STUDIOS

DISNEY/MGM STUDIOS OPENS
Hollywood Boulevard
The Great Movie Ride
Backstage Studio Tour
The Looney Bin
"Indiana Jones™ Epic Stunt Spectacular"
Superstar Television
The Monster Sound Show
Behind the Scenes Special Effects Tour
The Magic of Disney Animation
New York Street
'50s Prime Time Cafe
The Hollywood Brown Derby
Streetmosphere
Echo Lake

THE REST OF THE WORLD

PLEASURE ISLAND OPENS
Adventurers Club
Neon Armadillo
Comedy Warehouse
8 Trax
Mannequins Dance Palace
XZFR Rock 'n' Roll Beach Club

DISNEY'S TYPHOON LAGOON

TAKE FLIGHT

Currently called Take Flight, this attraction is like a childhood fantasy whisking guests into the pages of a giant pop-up book for a whimsical look at the adventure and romance of flight. Above, the sun sets over Paris rooftops; right, a humorous scene depicting the early days of aviation.

DISNEY CHARACTER HIT PARADE

All the favorite Disney characters joined in a rousing "Zip, Zip, Zip-A-Dee-Doo-Dah" performed by Disney's crowd-pleasing World Band, above. Colorful floats included *The Jungle Book,* left; *Little Mermaid,* with a grinning Flounder leading the way, bottom left; a menacing Captain Hook commanding his ship on the *Peter Pan* float, right; and Honest John, Gideon, Pinocchio, and Stromboli on the *Pinocchio* float, bottom right.

1989

EPCOT®

WONDERS OF LIFE

From a frenzied "flight" through the human body to a sensitive film about human reproduction, this 100,000-square-foot gold geodesic dome is designed to celebrate fitness, wellness, and the joy of being alive. Inside, the Fitness Fairgrounds give guests dozens of opportunities to learn firsthand about keeping fit, from an analysis of their golf swing to a virtual ride through the Rose Bowl Parade or Disneyland on a stationary Wonder Cycle. The relationship between mental and physical health is explored in Cranium Command, a lighthearted theater show in which the audience helps to "pilot" the brain of an adolescent boy.

Giant steel Tower of Life, above, a 76-foot, 25-ton tower based on the molecular structure of DNA, points the way to the Future World pavilion. Inside, Pluto takes a practice swing in Coaches Corner, left, where guests get tips from professionals in golf, tennis, and baseball, with instant video replays of their efforts.

Above left, guests try audio experiences in the Sensory Funhouse. Above right, Buzzy takes charge in Cranium Command. Goofy About Health, above, stars the lovable hound. Left, Body Wars, a thrill ride through the human body.

1989

DISNEY/MGM STUDIOS

From the moment guests enter Disney/MGM Studios, they feel as if they have strolled into the middle of the action. Thrilling movie and TV attractions throughout the park capture the larger-than-life spirit of Hollywood, starting with Hollywood Boulevard, a giant movie set straight out of the fabulous '30s and '40s. Inside the park, guests can get a peek at upcoming Disney animated features in The Magic of Disney Animation attraction and a chance to watch stars at work on soundstages and on sprawling backlot sets.

Far left, The Earffel Tower is the Studios' unforget-table landmark. Top, the massive Disney/MGM Studios gate leads the way to real-life filmmaking—the Disney/MGM Studios Backlot Tour and The Magic of Disney Animation. Left, the Chinese Theatre with a lavish production for a TV special. Above, Mickey and Minnie's hand- and footprints in the theatre's spacious courtyard.

HOLLYWOOD BOULEVARD

The glamour, excitement, and eccentricities of Hollywood in its heyday greet guests entering the Disney/MGM Studios, with the famous Chinese Theatre beckoning from the far end of the street. Real Hollywood buildings that flourished in the days of art deco show up on the street in idealized form, with stylized signs and elaborate ornamentation. Period automobiles, like the one shown at right, add to the fantasy.

1989

THE GREAT MOVIE RIDE

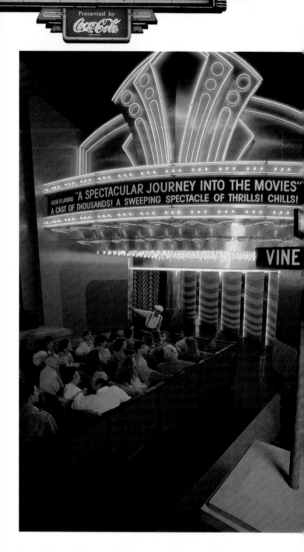

A replica of the world-famous Chinese Theatre, left, is the exterior of The Great Movie Ride, where your journey through some of the most famous films in silver-screen history starts under an old-fashioned theater marquee, above. Legendary movie stars, like James Cagney, John Wayne, Gene Kelly, Julie Andrews, and others, come to life in memorable performances, with edge-of-the-seat adventure in some of the more sinister scenes. All ends happily, of course, with a final scene from the *Wizard of Oz* and a grand finale film montage.

Familiar scenes from
Raiders of the Lost Ark,
Wizard of Oz, and
Casablanca.

1989

DISNEY/MGM STUDIOS BACKLOT TOUR

The backstage tour begins with a tram ride, above, past preproduction costuming quarters, scene shops, and along a residential backlot. Stops include Catastrophe Canyon, left, an exciting special-effects demonstration that surprises unsuspecting guests with an earthquake, oil-field fire, and a flash flood.

THE LOONY BIN

Special effects and plenty of hilarious props from the movie *Who Framed Roger Rabbit* kept guests entertained in the Loony Bin, closed in 1997 to make way for the Goosebumps™ HorrorLand Fright Show and FunHouse.

"Indiana Jones™ Epic Stunt Spectacular"

Stunt performers brave earth-shattering crashes and fiery explosions to thrill guests visiting this attraction, which re-creates scenes from the blockbuster film *Raiders of the Lost Ark*. Indy barely escapes a giant stone ball, below left, and the flames are hot enough for the audience to feel as Indiana saves Marion, below, from the machine-gun fire of German soldiers and an out-of-control truck that explodes on impact.

1989

SUPERSTAR TELEVISION

SuperStar is rollicking fun that transforms park guests into actors, using today's electronic technology to put them into some of the best television shows of all time, from TV's live bloopers and blunders in the '50s to late-night, modern-day antics.

THE MONSTER SOUND SHOW

Dozens of crazy contraptions and thinga-majigs, each capable of producing a distinctive sound, become the tools of fledgling "audio artists" selected from the audience. A live-action comedy horror short was the film used until 1997, when the Monster Sound Show became the ABC Sound Studio. Now audience members add sound effects to kids' shows from the ABC-TV Saturday morning lineup—with results that are hilarious.

BEHIND THE SCENES SPECIAL-EFFECTS TOUR

Above, a revolving series of exhibits based on popular Disney films shows how film is shot against a blue screen so it can be superimposed onto any background, like this scene featuring guests and a giant bee from the hit film *Honey, I Shrunk the Kids*. Left, a young volunteer gets drenched in a make-believe storm at sea in the special-effects water tank.

1989····

THE MAGIC OF DISNEY ANIMATION

Guests get a front-row seat through glass walls at the world's only animation facility featuring a visitor tour. Animators create the drawings that will appear in real films, like the artist, top right, working to give the hyena character in *The Lion King* a grin

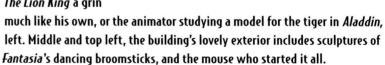

much like his own, or the animator studying a model for the tiger in *Aladdin*, left. Middle and top left, the building's lovely exterior includes sculptures of *Fantasia*'s dancing broomsticks, and the mouse who started it all.

NEW YORK STREET

It's Disney's version of the Big Apple, where stars and crews are at work on projects for producers from around the world. Far left, this traffic jam may look like it goes on for miles, but it's just two city blocks —the skyscrapers, actually painted flats, provide an example of forced perspective. Left, filming a musical sequence for a TV special about the opening of the studio.

1989

50's Prime Time Cafe

Formica tables, kitschy knickknacks and black-and-white TVs tuned to classic oldies give Prime Time, left, a '50s feel. The Hollywood Brown Derby, below, is a re-creation of the former Tinseltown mainstay, right down to the celebrity caricatures on the walls.

The Hollywood Brown Derby

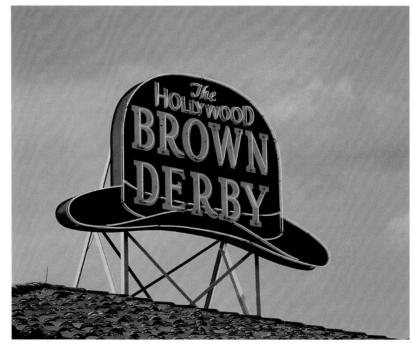

STREETMOSPHERE

Kooky "Streetmosphere" character actors—detectives, starlets, cabbies, cops, and even a gossip columnist—bring to life the glamour, excitement, and eccentricities of Hollywood in its youngest and least pretentious era. Guests may find themselves in the middle of the action, when Disney actors playing the role of directors set out to "discover" fresh talent straight from the streets.

ECHO LAKE

Echo Lake is a real place in Los Angeles, and this re-creation at the Disney/MGM Studios is home to Dinosaur Gertie's Ice Creams of Extinction, a classic example of "California Crazy" roadside architecture of the '40s. Across the water is Min & Bill's Dockside Diner, a tramp steamer based on the 1930 film.

1989

THE REST OF THE WORLD

PLEASURE ISLAND OPENS

In the Disney tradition of great storytelling, Pleasure Island started with a very tall tale about the discovery of an abandoned shipbuilding operation of an adventuresome entrepreneur named Merriweather Adam Pleasure. According to the legend, Pleasure and his two sons built quite an empire, beginning in the late 19th century and continuing for nearly 60 years until bad business decisions and a destructive hurricane in the 1950s left the place in shambles.

Thirty years later, Disney designers discovered the waterfront ruins and decided to restore the place, converting the warehouse-style buildings into high-energy nightclubs, boutiques, and restaurants to create a six-acre entertainment complex.

Now part of the *Downtown Disney* area, Pleasure Island comes alive each evening with a street party and tribute to New Year's Eve, complete with fireworks and confetti. The entertainment continues in assorted clubs, all housed in the buildings that once were part of Pleasure's flourishing empire.

Pleasure Island lights up when the sun goes down, with a wild New Year's Eve finale every night on the famed West End Stage, above. Three footbridges, like the one above right, conveniently connect the island to the mainland. Besides the night-clubs, there are ultra-plush movie theaters, restaurants, and an unusual variety of shops that sell everything from trendy fashions to music memorabilia.

1989

PLEASURE ISLAND

A revolving dance floor and light show create an exuberant atmosphere in Mannequins Dance Palace, left, with actual mannequins that give the illusion of a giant theatrical warehouse. Below left, XZFR Rock 'n' Roll Beach Club, with live bands performing hits from the '50s to the present, and below right, 8Trax (originally Videopolis East), where guests dance to sounds from the disco era.

Clockwise from top left: Comedy Warehouse troupe, the stage show in Adventurers Club, Island Explosion Dancers on West End Stage, live music at Neon Armadillo Music Saloon (which closed in summer 1997 to make way for BET Soundstage Club in 1998), and spontaneous acting in Adventurers Club.

1989

Disney's Typhoon Lagoon

Like a surfside playground left behind by a great storm, Disney's Typhoon Lagoon ushers in a new generation of water adventures for Walt Disney World® Resort guests. The park is designed to look like a ramshackle, tin-roofed island village, with Mt. Mayday towering behind, landscaped with water slides and topped with a shipwrecked shrimp boat named *Miss Tilly*—left dangling 95 feet in the air by the force of the legendary typhoon.

Encircling the lagoon is Castaway Creek, top left, offering a relaxing inner tube ride. Right, snorkelers swim fin to fin with exotic marine life, including nurse sharks, in Shark Reef.

STAY CLEAR
OF PROPELLOR

1989

1983·1988

MAGIC KINGDOM® PARK

MICKEY'S BIRTHDAYLAND (1988)

EVENTS
> MICKEY'S 60TH BIRTHDAY CELEBRATION (1988)
> WALT DISNEY WORLD VERY MERRY
>   CHRISTMAS PARADE (1983)
> DONALD DUCK'S 50TH BIRTHDAY PARADE (1984)
> 15TH ANNIVERSARY CELEBRATION (1986)

EPCOT®

FUTURE WORLD
> JOURNEY INTO IMAGINATION (1983)
> HORIZONS (1983)
> THE LIVING SEAS (1986)

WORLD SHOWCASE
> MOROCCO (1984)
> NORWAY (1988)
> ILLUMINATIONS (1988)

BE OUR GUEST

> DISNEY'S GRAND FLORIDIAN BEACH RESORT &
>   SPA (1988)
> DISNEY'S CARIBBEAN BEACH RESORT (1988)

MICKEY'S 60TH BIRTHDAY CELEBRATION

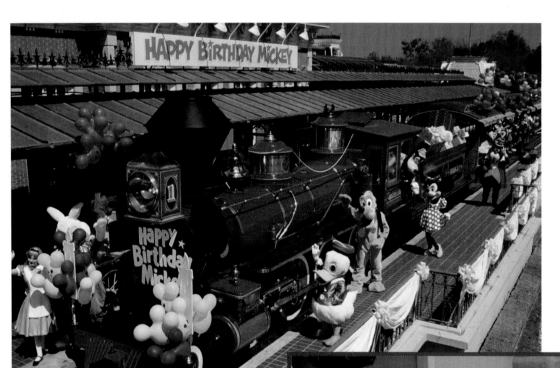

The Magic Kingdom Park was decked out to celebrate Mickey's 60th birthday, from the train station to a whole new land, Mickey's Birthdayland, where Minnie Moo showed off her distinctive silhouette, below left, while Minnie and Mickey greeted fans—or took a spin in Mickey's shiny red car.

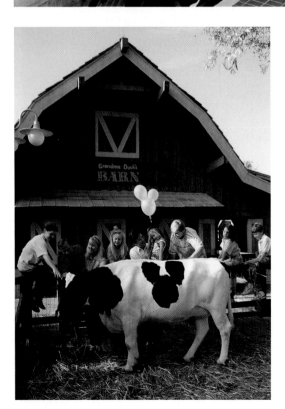

As a birthday card for Mickey, a Sheffield, Iowa, family planted 240 acres of corn—6 million plants—edged in oats to artfully resemble the Big Cheese, top. Above and right, interiors of Mickey's new digs in Birthdayland.

DID YOU KNOW?

Mickey Mouse has more then 150 sets of clothes to choose from when he gets dressed, from his familiar black jacket, yellow bow tie, and red pants to a wet suit for scuba diving. But Minnie Mouse has him beat—she selects from a closet of more than 175 different ensembles, including several sequined evening gowns, bathing suits, miniskirts, even an African dashiki.

WALT DISNEY WORLD VERY MERRY CHRISTMAS PARADE

Life-size toy soldiers and giant gingerbread boys and girls make their way down Main Street U.S.A., in this magical holiday parade, an annual Magic Kingdom® tradition. The parade debuted in 1983 with hosts Joan Lunden and Mike Douglas.

DONALD'S 50TH BIRTHDAY PARADE

Finally, a delighted Donald Duck starred in his very own parade in 1984, celebrating his 50th birthday. And not just Donald, but 50 more quacking compatriots kept him company in the inaugural birthday parade, along with Clarence "Ducky" Nash, the voice of Donald.

15th Anniversary Parade

A giant celebration kicked off in October 1986, with Mickey and Minnie hosting the daily parade. Mickey's fancy pyrotechnic fingers wowed Magic Kingdom® guests, and there was no time but party time during the yearlong gala.

EPCOT®

JOURNEY INTO IMAGINATION

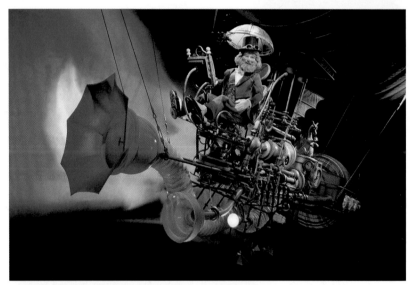

Wise, jolly Dreamfinder and his tiny purple dragon, named Figment, are the hosts in this delightful attraction, which includes a ride through the world of imagination, above and left, and Image Works, top left, an electronic playground full of experiences designed to give guests the chance to use their imaginations, like the neon Rainbow Corridor.

Stunning nighttime view of Imagination pavilion, above, shows two towering pyramids made of triangles of mirrored glass. More magic in the ride-through attraction, left. The pavilion's Magic Eye Theater opened in 1983 with the 3-D *Magic Journeys*. In 1986 it premiered *Captain EO*, which was replaced with *Honey, I Shrunk the Audience* in 1994.

1983
1988

HORIZONS

Domestic robots, left and right, are fanciful by today's standards, yet these early visions renew hope for the next century's inventive process in this pavilion, which looks into the achievable future and takes guests on an exciting exploration of options for living and working in the 21st century—to Nova Cite, an urban space center; Mesa Verde, a desert farming community; and Sea Castle, an underwater city. The lyrics of "Horizons" (the attractions theme song) remind guests that, "if we can dream it, we can do it."

Future cities, left and above, show the human side of life in the future —a holographic telephone for keeping in touch and a gravity-free stroll in a free-floating space colony.

1983
1988

THE LIVING SEAS

Containing the world's sixth-largest ocean, albeit manmade, this pavilion is dedicated to our relationship with the underwater world. More than 4,000 sea creatures, including sharks, parrot fish, rays, dolphins—and even Mickey Mouse on occasion—inhabit the coral reef in the 5.6-million-gallon tank. Guests visit Sea Base Alpha, right and below, an undersea research facility where they can see the divers live and up close carrying out research with marine mammals.

1983
1988

Morocco

Moroccan artisans spent months creating the detailed geometric patterns in the buildings, like the Koutoubia Minaret, right, a re-creation of the famous prayer tower in Marrakesh that stands guard over the entrance to the Morocco pavilion. The Medina, or old city, above, lets guests experi-ence the feeling of a bustling Moroccan marketplace. Restaurant Marrakesh, below right, offers popular Moroccan dishes and features belly dancers, accompanied by a genuine Moroccan string band.

Norway

Picturesque Norway features Maelstrom, a fantasy voyage aboard small ships, bottom left, patterned after the dragon-headed craft of Eric the Red. The boats slip into the shadows of a mythical Norwegian forest where a troll casts a spell on the boat, below. Young Norwegians on yearlong internships, middle and bottom, work in the pavilion.

ILLUMINATIONS

This nighttime spectacular, regarded as an attraction in itself, features fireworks, fountains, lights, and lasers that light up World Showcase Lagoon and the surrounding countries to the accompaniment of symphonic music. Each country gets a burst of color with thousands of tiny lights, like China, far left; Canada, left; France, below left; and United Kingdom, below right. More than 100 rainbow-colored fountains soar 40 feet high, and a dozen show barges shoot 835 fireworks rockets—totaling at least 304,775 blasts a year—making it a breathtaking celebration every night. A massive laser projection on Spaceship Earth is the show's finale.

1983
1988

BE OUR GUEST

DISNEY'S GRAND FLORIDIAN BEACH RESORT & SPA

The "crown jewel" of Disney's resorts, this 900-room Victorian structure recalls the grandeur of fancy seashore getaways in the late 1900s. The main building's palatial lobby, left, is a show-stopper, with stained-glass domes in the ceiling, an aviary, and an old-fashioned open-cage elevator to the second-floor shops and monorail station. Situated on the shores of Seven Seas Lagoon, the resort offers several rooms with views of Cinderella Castle.

DISNEY'S CARIBBEAN BEACH RESORT

Fabulous, sun-washed colors of the Caribbean give this 500-acre resort a tropical feel. Five villages—Martinique, Trinidad, Jamaica, Aruba, and Barbados—surround a 45-acre lake, left, and a lakeside recreation area, bottom, that includes a meandering pool with waterfalls and slides, an island playground, and a wildlife trail.

1983
1988

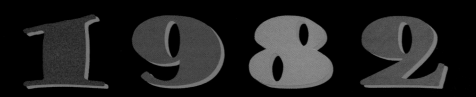

1982

EPCOT® OPENS

FUTURE WORLD
- SPACESHIP EARTH
- COMMUNICORE
- THE LAND
- UNIVERSE OF ENERGY
- WORLD OF MOTION

WORLD SHOWCASE
- MEXICO
- CHINA
- GERMANY
- ITALY
- AMERICAN ADVENTURE
- JAPAN
- FRANCE
- UNITED KINGDOM
- CANADA

EPCOT® (FUTURE WORLD)

OPENING DAY

Thousands gathered for their first glimpse of Epcot on October 1, 1982, the beginning of opening-month festivities that included performances by artists from 23 countries around the world. "Epcot is inspired by Walt Disney's creative genius. Here, human achievements are celebrated through imagination, the wonders of enterprise, and concepts of a future that promise new and exciting benefits for all," the dedication proclaims. Nicknamed "the living blueprint of the future," Epcot continues to entertain, inform, and inspire.

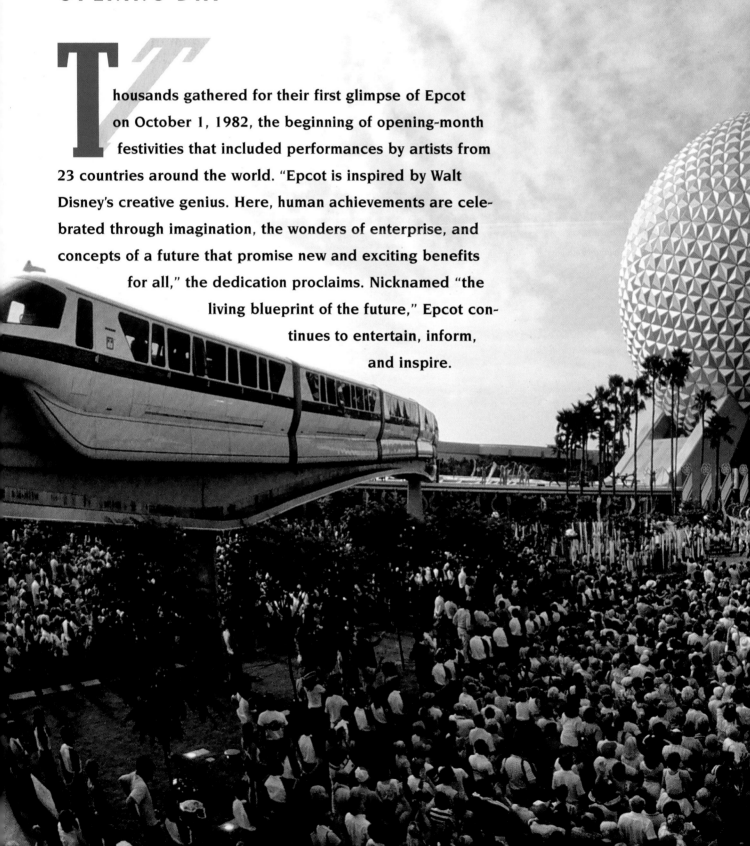

Spaceship Earth was the perfect backdrop for 21st-century-themed entertainment. Throughout opening month, hundreds of dignitaries, including Walt Disney's wife, Lillian, experienced the wonders of Future World and World Showcase.

1982

SPACESHIP EARTH

An amazing journey through time
starts with the caveman's earliest
attempts to communicate, above,
and ends with scenes of 21st-century
networking that ties the world
together, below.

Along the way, elabo-
rate scenes, like the
Greek theater, above,
an Italian Renaissance
scene, left, and a life-
size Michelangelo
painting the ceiling of
the Sistine Chapel,
below, trace the story
of the evolution of
human communication.

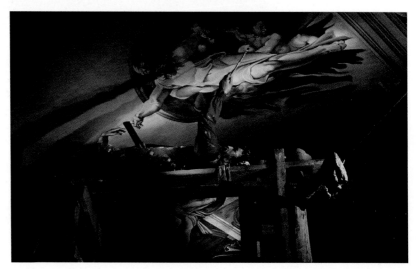

This landmark Epcot® attraction is the world's only geosphere, standing 180 feet high and created with 954 shiny aluminum panels. Inset shows the WorldKey communications system that was part of the pavilion before its recent renovation; WorldKey still exists in kiosks throughout the park.

1982

COMMUNICORE

Turn one direction and learn about computers; turn another and preview a vacation spot anywhere in the world. Communicore East and Communicore West, two crescent-shaped buildings in the heart of Future World, explored modern-day technology with interactive exhibits, like the amusing Network Control game, top right, that lets guests try their hand at routing long-distance telephone calls. Right center, guests turned cranks to light up the bulbs, and a purple robot named SMRT-1 played guessing games. Below, an overview of Communicore East. In July 1994, Communicore became Innoventions.

ELECTRONIC MAIL

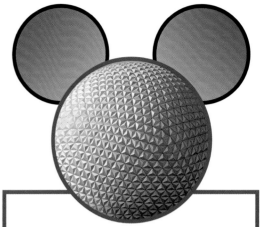

DID YOU KNOW?

Many Walt Disney World® Resort guests say that Spaceship Earth looks like a giant golf ball. If the 180-foot-tall geosphere were a golf ball, the hole would have to be about 417 feet in diameter, and the golfer would have to be more than a mile tall. And if he were playing on the equivalent of a 200-yard hole, it would be nearly 134 miles long—approximately the width of Florida.

More Communicore exhibits, including Electronic Forum, where guests could give their opinions on current issues in an ongoing, computerized poll.

1982

THE LAND

This enormous pavilion spreads over six acres at Epcot®, and offers an entertaining look at the foods we eat. In Listen to the Land, above, a fantastic boat ride takes guests through greenhouses full of living crops, showcasing futuristic growing methods.

Left, the miracle of photosynthesis is captured in this fantasy creation in Listen to the Land. Patio umbrellas, opposite page, brighten the Farmers Market, the pavilion's casual food court.

Kitchen Kabaret

Kitchen Kabaret, the original stage show in The Land, featured an endearing cast of fruit and veggies in a musical about good nutrition. Mr. Eggz, middle left, cracked more than his share of corny jokes, along with Mr. Hamm, below. The show closed in 1994 to make way for Food Rocks.

Universe of Energy

Lifelike dinosaurs make this a favorite Epcot® attraction, as guests journey back to prehistoric times to learn about the importance of energy. The striking pavilion's roof is covered with two acres of photovoltaic cells that convert sunlight to electricity to help power the attraction.

1982

WORLD OF MOTION

The story of transportation past, present, and future was presented in this wheel-shaped, stainless-steel-clad pavilion. Closed in 1996 to make way for the new Test Track, World of Motion took guests from the early days of sailing, flying, and two-wheel transportation, opposite page bottom, to the elaborate city scene, top, where old and new collided on a busy street corner. From there it was a fast-paced journey to a city of the future, with visions of flying cars. The latest-model General Motors autos and prototypes were at the conclusion of the ride in the Transcenter, where guests could climb behind the wheel of a brand-new car or take a sneak peek at future models.

DID YOU KNOW?

What is the most photographed spot at Epcot®? Not Spaceship Earth, but the model cars and prototypes, housed at the General Motors pavilion.

1982....

EPCOT® (WORLD SHOWCASE)

There is no passport required for this whirlwind trip to 11 nations around the globe: familiar architecture, historic scenes, and magnificent landscapes are designed to suggest an authentic experience in each village, all linked on a wide promenade around World Showcase Lagoon. Friendly cultural ambassadors help guests get acquainted in each of the countries, where exotic cuisine, entertainment, and artisans complete the global experience.

MEXICO

An impressive pyramid, far left, sets the stage for a visit to Mexico, where inside the pavilion "El Río del Tiempo" takes guests on a leisurely boat ride through the country's colorful history. Diners in the enchanting San Angel Inn, below, get a front-row seat as the boats pass by a mystical pyramid and smoking volcano, below. The pavilion also includes a lively marketplace with authentic Mexican wares, from sombreros to piñatas.

1982

CHINA

Serene gardens and the ornate Temple of Heaven, left , inspired by the original in Beijing, create one of the loveliest World Showcase villages. Inside, the CircleVision 360 presentation, *Wonders of China: Land of Beauty, Land of Time,* includes scenes never before captured on film. Below, agile stilt walkers entertain in the courtyard.

GERMANY

The architecture, right out of a fairy tale, include these charming figurines, below, which help chime the giant glockenspiel in the cobblestone-paved central plaza.

Guests get a rousing welcome, above, on their way to the boisterous Biergarten restaurant, center, offering German specialties along with lively music.

1982

ITALY

Elegant architecture that includes Bernini's Neptune fountain, right, and a version of the Campanile of St. Mark's Square in Venice, above, gives a taste of Italy's major sites. The piazza is alive with colorful entertainers, middle right, and mouth-watering food at L'Originale Alfredo di Roma, top right .

FRANCE

This postcard-perfect village includes a wonderful restaurant run by three of France's legendary chefs, Gaston Lenôtre, Roger Verge, and Paul Bocuse, left to right below. The pavilion's film, *Impressions de France*, is filled with the beauty of the nation.

1982

UNITED KINGDOM

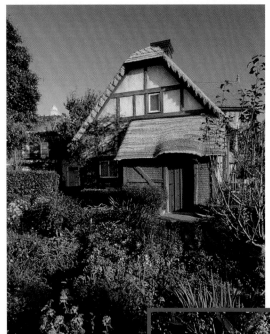

Guests traverse the British Isles, from the thatched-roof cottages in the English countryside, above and right, to a city square, top, where the comedic Pearlies, so named for the decorative buttons on their costumes, entertain.

Formal British ceremonies, including a show of the Union Jack, above, were part of the monthlong festivities for the opening of Epcot® that included festive traditions from the nine World Showcase countries that opened in 1982.

CANADA

Offering a broad sweep across our neighbor to the north, the Canada pavilion includes totem poles from the Northwest, right, and the towering Hotel du Canada, center left, inspired by Ottawa's Château Laurier. Entertainment, too, borrows from diverse regions, including bagpipes from the Maritimes, above. There's even a humorous Canadian Mountie patrolling the promenade, bottom left.

1982

1972/1981

MAGIC KINGDOM® PARK

MAIN STREET U.S.A.
The Walt Disney Story (1972)
Swan Boats (1972)

TOMORROWLAND
If You Had Wings (1972)
Carousel of Progress (1972)
Star Jets (1974)
WEDway People Mover (1975)
Space Mountain (1975)

ADVENTURELAND
Pirates of the Caribbean (1973)

FRONTIERLAND
Tom Sawyer Island (1973)
Richard F. Irvine Steamboat (1975)
Big Thunder Mountain Railroad (1980)

EVENTS
Main Street Electrical Parade (1977)
Mickey's 50th Birthday Celebration (1978)
Tencennial Celebration (1981)
Happy Easter Parade (1972)
America on Parade (1975)

BE OUR GUEST

Disney's Golf Resort (1973)

THE REST OF THE WORLD

DISNEY'S DISCOVERY ISLAND (1974)

DISNEY VILLAGE MARKETPLACE (1975)

RIVER COUNTRY (1976)

THE WALT DISNEY STORY

Walt himself narrated part of this presentation, which opened in a building on the east side of Town Square in 1973, telling the story of the great man who built a kingdom around a mouse. The attraction closed in 1992.

SWAN BOATS

Fifteen of these 30-passenger boats made their maiden voyages in 1973 on the Magic Kingdom waterways. Departing from a dock in front of Cinderella Castle, the boats circumnavigated Adventureland, Liberty Square, Fantasyland, and Tomorrowland. The Swan Boats closed in 1983.

IF YOU HAD WINGS

This Tomorrowland attraction, which opened in 1972, lets guests climb aboard for a trip to exotic locales around the globe. It was eventually replaced by Take Flight, the current attraction.

CAROUSEL OF PROGRESS

A longtime Tomorrowland favorite, Carousel of Progress originally was an attraction at the 1964-65 New York World's Fair. The Walt Disney World version opened in 1973, with the theme song, "The Best Time of Your Life."

1972
1981

StarJets/WEDway People Mover

StarJets, below, started flying above Tomorrowland in 1974. They were replaced with Astro Orbiter in 1994. In 1975, the WEDway People Mover (renamed Tomorrowland Transit Authority in 1994), inset opposite page, added another attraction, with an elevated track that offers a leisurely way to view most of the major Tomorrowland attractions. The PeopleMover also shows off an innovative means of transportation, operated by a linear induction motor that has no moving parts, uses little power, and emits no pollution.

EXIT

1972
1981

SPACE MOUNTAIN

Mickey Mouse hosted the debut of this Tomorrowland thrill ride in 1972, above. The Disney version of a roller coaster starts with speed-tunnel special effects, then twists and turns in the dark, catching riders by surprise as they zip past comets and shooting stars in outer space. The original ride vehicles, below, were replaced with newer versions in 1989.

DID YOU KNOW?

False teeth, wigs, wallets, and eyeglasses... hold on to your belongings, because all of these and more have been found at the bottom of the track in Space Mountain, lost by guests caught off guard as the thrill ride hurtles them through the darkness. But don't worry: Disney's Lost & Found keeps track of the belongings until they are retrieved.

The gleaming white building that houses Space Mountain, considered futuristic when it was designed in the 1970s, rises 180 feet and is 300 feet in diameter.

1972
1981

PIRATES OF THE CARIBBEAN

A crowd-pleaser at Disneyland, the Walt Disney World version of Pirates of the Caribbean opened in 1973 in Caribbean Plaza, an expansion of Adventureland. A clock tower marks the entrance, opposite page. In one of the longest and most elaborate Magic Kingdom® attractions, guests sail by flying cannonballs and a buried treasure as Audio-Animatronic pirates comically plunder a Caribbean town—all to the familiar sounds of "Yo Ho (a Pirate's Life for Me)."

1972
1981

Tom Sawyer Island

This island attraction opened in the middle of the Rivers of America in 1973. The island is reached by taking a raft, bottom right, from Frontierland. The bouncing barrel bridge, left, is one of the low-key adventures on the way to Fort Sam Clemens, below, which has great views from the second floor.

RICHARD F. IRVINE STEAMBOAT

Steam helps turn the huge paddlewheel on the Liberty Square riverboat, named for Dick Irvine, one of Disney's early designers. The pleasant journey is a great way to relax any time of the day as it takes guests on a scenic trip along the Rivers of America.

Big Thunder Mountain Railroad

Another Disney-made mountain opened in 1980, this one set in a Southwestern landscape reminiscent of the windswept terrain found in Arizona's Monument Valley. The runaway train whips around the roller-coaster curves and down deep gorges, barely giving guests enough time to take in the amusing, realistic details that re-create the gold rush era of the Old West, including the little town of Tumbleweed in the middle of a flash flood. Crashing landslides, rumbling earthquakes, and dark caverns add to the excitement.

1972
1981

MAIN STREET ELECTRICAL PARADE

The first nighttime Magic Kingdom® parade premiered in 1977 to rave reviews. Main Street U.S.A., was illuminated with a million twinkling lights while guests tapped their toes to the accompanying "Baroque Hoedown." The Disney characters were all there, including a gigantic Pete's Dragon, bottom. SpectroMagic replaced the parade in 1991, and now the Electrical Parade is at The Disneyland Paris Park.

MICKEY'S 50TH BIRTHDAY CELEBRATION

Mickey Mouse celebrated his 50th birthday in high style in 1978, with a special parade down Main Street U.S.A. Then, stepping out with Minnie Mouse, he commemorated the world premiere of his very first film, *Steamboat Willie*—first released at the Colony Theater in New York on November 18, 1928.

Tencennial Celebration

October 1, 1981, kicked off a yearlong celebration of the 10th anniversary of the Walt Disney World® Resort. Cast members created a giant "10" in front of Cinderella Castle, left, and hot-air balloons floated in the evening skies over the Seven Seas Lagoon, top.

HAPPY EASTER PARADE

The first Happy Easter parade down Main Street U.S.A., occurred in 1972. The parade has become an annual tradition in the Magic Kingdom® Park, now televised with celebrity hosts joining Mickey and Minnie Mouse in their springtime finery.

AMERICA ON PARADE

The joyous red, white, and blue America on Parade kicked off in 1975, left, and ran for two years with Mickey, Goofy, and Donald reprising the fife and drum corps, above.

**1972
1981**

BE OUR GUEST

DISNEY'S GOLF RESORT

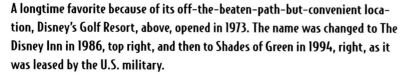

A longtime favorite because of its off-the-beaten-path-but-convenient location, Disney's Golf Resort, above, opened in 1973. The name was changed to The Disney Inn in 1986, top right, and then to Shades of Green in 1994, right, as it was leased by the U.S. military.

THE REST OF THE WORLD

DISNEY'S DISCOVERY ISLAND

In 1974 Disney opened a nature preserve on this 11-acre paradise, called Treasure Island. The name was changed to Discovery Island in 1977, when it was recognized as an accredited zoological park with a collection of more than 130 species of birds, mammals, reptiles, amphibians, and invertebrates, including the giant tortoises, far left.

1972
1981

DISNEY VILLAGE MARKETPLACE

The grand opening in 1975 of Disney Village Marketplace, now *Downtown Disney* Marketplace, along the shores of Buena Vista Lagoon included Cinderella and friends, left and above.

Among favorite accommodations in the area are the treehouse villas, left and above, which opened in 1972. These two-story octagonal houses on stilts are nestled in the woods, where bunnies and an occasional deer may be seen roaming in the early morning or late afternoon. Golf carts are provided for easy transportation around the area.

DISNEY'S RIVER COUNTRY WATER PARK

Disney's old-fashioned swimming hole opened in 1976 at Disney's Fort Wilderness Resort and Campground, actually a themed water park in a cove on Bay Lake. Guests can slip and slide down flumes, right and below, swing off ropes or a ship's boom, top right, or just relax on the white-sand beach.

1972
1981

1971

MAGIC KINGDOM® PARK

MAGIC KINGDOM PARK OPENS

MAIN STREET U.S.A.
- Walt Disney World Railroad
- Main Street Cinema
- The Crystal Palace

ADVENTURELAND
- Jungle Cruise
- Swiss Family Treehouse
- Tropical Serenade

FRONTIERLAND
- Country Bear Jamboree
- Diamond Horseshoe Saloon Revue
- Mike Fink Keelboats
- Davy Crockett's Explorer Canoes

LIBERTY SQUARE
- The Hall of Presidents
- The Liberty Tree
- The Haunted Mansion

FANTASYLAND
- Cinderella's Golden Carrousel
- Skyway to Tomorrowland
- Cinderella Castle
- Dumbo the Flying Elephant
- Mad Tea Party
- Mickey Mouse Revue
- Peter Pan's Flight
- Snow White's Scary Adventure
- Mr. Toad's Wild Ride
- It's a Small World
- 20,000 Leagues Under the Sea

TOMORROWLAND
- Grand Prix Raceway
- Flight to the Moon
- America the Beautiful

EVENTS
- Electrical Water Pageant
- Fantasy in the Sky Fireworks

BE OUR GUEST

- Disney's Contemporary Resort
- Disney's Polynesian Resort
- Disney's Fort Wilderness Resort & Campground

THE REST OF THE WORLD

DISNEY'S DINNER SHOWS

OPENING DAY

There was a liberal sprinkling of pixie dust as the Magic Kingdom Park celebrated its grand opening with the glorious sounds of a 1,076-piece marching band down Main Street U.S.A. "May Walt Disney World bring Joy and Inspiration and New Knowledge to all who come to this happy place…" said Walt's brother, Roy O. Disney, at the formal dedication on October 25, 1971.

The enormous construction project, unprecedented in Florida, took two years and about 9,000 workers to complete.

"Walt Disney World is a tribute to the philosophy and life of Walter Elias Disney and to the talents, the dedication, and loyalty of the entire Disney organization," said Roy O. Disney, left.

1971

Main Street U.S.A.

This enchanting street takes guests back to carefree, turn-of-the-century times, to a town that existed only in the daydreams of Walt Disney. There is an amazing mix of sensory delights— the sweet harmonies of a barbershop quartet, the clanging of the bell on a horse-drawn streetcar, the smell of fresh-baked cookies, the brilliant flowers spilling from their pots. And each block is a shopper's delight, displaying every imaginable sort of keepsake.

Victorian architecture and landscaping create a charming small-town ambience, left. Stylized signs, above, lend an old-fashioned air to the shops and carts along the bustling street (though the Penny Arcade is now gone).

The House of Magic, top left, which closed in 1995 to become part of the Main Street Athletic Club, was a favorite shop for tricks of the magician's trade. Horse-drawn trolley cars, above, shared Main Street U.S.A., with the omnibus, center left; the omnibus is no longer there, having been replaced by "horseless carriages" in the early 1980s. As the sun sets, this showplace becomes even more magical, with tiny lights edging all of the rooflines and the spectacular glow of Cinderella Castle.

1971....

WALT DISNEY WORLD RAILROAD

This grand railroad terminal creates a memorable entrance to the Magic Kingdom® Park, but it's also a working station, where passengers board one of four locomotives for a relaxing journey on the tracks that loop around the park. The steam-powered trains are originals that were discovered in the Yucatan.

MAIN STREET CINEMA

There's nothing like a cool, dark movie theater, and this one is special: the feature attraction is *Mickey's Big Break*, showing how Mickey is chosen for his first starring role. Other vintage cartoons follow, including *Steamboat Willie*, the first Mickey Mouse cartoon released.

DID YOU KNOW?

Glance upward—above Main Street's "shopkeeper" windows—to see various names etched into second-story window signs, where Disney places the names of honored employees and others connected with the company. Of all the names highlighted, only one painted window faces Cinderella Castle: "Walter E. Disney Graduate School of Design and Master Planning" (it's above the ice cream shop).

THE CRYSTAL PALACE

This landmark restaurant is one of the prettiest buildings in the Magic Kingdom® Park. Guests dine here in a Victorian-style garden setting, with fresh flowers in hanging baskets and glorious views of the surrounding flower beds and a secluded courtyard.

1971

ADVENTURELAND

Lush landscaping and distinctive architecture from the South Seas, Caribbean, Polynesia, and Southeast Asia create this exotic land, where the mysterious sound of beating jungle drums and the distant boom of a cannon entice guests to exciting adventures.

Giant carvings, above and top, add to the ambience. The dramatic architecture of Adventureland was inspired by Walt Disney's True-Life Adventure series, which he produced at remote locations around the globe.

JUNGLE CRUISE

A humorous skipper keeps this trip light-hearted as guests venture to colorful, far-away places aboard an exciting cruise. Bathing elephants, fierce tigers, jungle snakes, and other realistic creatures are discovered along the way, with a Cambodian temple, bottom right, among the mysterious sights.

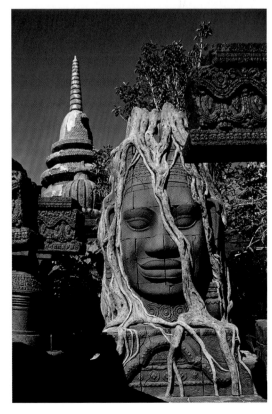

Swiss Family Treehouse

Guests can climb 116 steps to the farthest reaches of this giant tree, inspired by the Robinson family's elaborate treehouse in the classic book and 1960 Disney film, complete with lovely mahogany furniture, a pump organ, comfortable bedrooms, and even running water. Resembling a banyan tree, the steel, concrete, and stucco structure—unofficially christened *Disneyodendron eximus*, or "out-of-the-ordinary Disney tree"—weighs 200 tons and is covered with 300,000 polyethylene leaves on 1,400 branches.

Tropical Serenade

Among the first of the Audio-Animatronic attractions, the enchanted Tiki birds were joined by more than 200 of their feathered friends, tropical flowers, and tiki god statues singing and whistling the unforgettable "Tiki Room" theme song. The attraction closed in September 1997, and is to reopen in March 1998 with "classic birdbrains from recent Disney features."

1971

FRONTIERLAND

Walt Disney always was interested in the country's western heritage, and this exciting land transports guests back 200 years to the colorful days of the American frontier, stretching from the rugged Wild West to the charming Old South. Ghost towns and boomtowns come to life to celebrate the spirit of a simpler, carefree era.

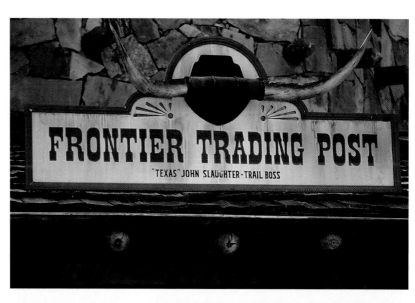

The desertlike landscape helps re-create the Wild West, where the cactus forms a silhouette of mouse ears, right. Stylized sign, above, leads the way to the Pecos Bill Cafe for burgers and barbecued chicken.

COUNTRY BEAR JAMBOREE

More than 20 lovable, life-size Audio-Animatronic bears entertain with an amusing medley of songs in this witty stage show at Grizzly Hall, starring favorites like Big Al, Liver-Lips, McGrowl, and Teddi Barra.

1971

Diamond Horseshoe Saloon Revue

Corny jokes and an energetic cast of can-can dancers have been the hallmarks of this popular western revue since its grand opening on October 1, 1971. The original show ran until it was changed on October 1, 1986, when it became the Diamond Horseshoe Jamboree.

Mike Fink Keelboats

The two boats, named *Bertha Mae* and *Gullywhumper*, offer a leisurely ride on the Rivers of America, left. The attraction is based on the Disney television episode, "Davy Crockett's Keel Boat Race," where Davy raced the *Bertha Mae* against Mike Fink's *Gullywhumper*.

Davy Crockett's Explorer Canoes

Although now gone, these canoes were in Frontierland on opening day in 1971, and guests really paddled the 35-foot-long boats through the Rivers of America circling Tom Sawyer Island, past moose, deer, Indian settlements, log cabins, and other reminders of the American frontier.

LIBERTY SQUARE

The architectural splendor of Colonial America is re-created in beautiful Liberty Square. The centerpiece is the majestic Liberty Tree, decorated with 13 lanterns, representing the original 13 colonies.

In 1971, guests could get a fascinating history lesson in the Hall of Presidents or encounter 999 grinning ghosts in the frightfully funny Haunted Mansion.

THE HALL OF PRESIDENTS

Originally, President Abraham Lincoln, left, had the only speaking role in this popular attraction. The realistic Audio-Animatronic figures nod, fidget, even whisper amongst themselves as the story of the Constitution unfolds. Disney artists give new meaning to the term "head of state," below.

THE LIBERTY TREE

The Liberty Tree, decorated with its 13 lanterns, is a 35-ton, 40-foot-high live oak, which was transplanted from the southern edge of Walt Disney World® Resort. It is estimated to be 135 years old.

1971

THE HAUNTED MANSION

Startling special effects bring the spooky specters to life for an evening of merriment, above and top right. Ghostly spirits cause a stir in the graveyard, center right. In the finale, a friendly phantom catches a ride with surprised guests, right.

The elaborate dining hall is one of the most amazing scenes in the old house. The mansion itself, inset, is modeled after mansions built by the Dutch in the 18th century in the Hudson River valley.

1971

FANTASYLAND

The most enchanting Magic Kingdom® land has the spirit of a lively Renaissance fair, where favorite characters from Disney classics magically come to life. Children of all ages can fly away with the lovable Dumbo or mischievous Peter Pan, or step into the timeless tales of Cinderella and Snow White. They can get lost on the road to Nowhere in Particular on Mr. Toad's Wild Ride, or spin wildly out of control in the oversized teacups inspired by *Alice in Wonderland*. Best of all, there's always a happy ending.

The architecture, too, is straight out of a fairytale, with quick-service restaurants, like the Pinocchio Village Haus, above, and shops housed in charming re-creations of European buildings.

1971

CINDERELLA'S GOLDEN CARROUSEL

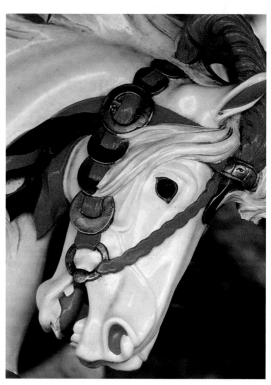

SKYWAY TO TOMORROWLAND

Built in 1917 and discovered in Olympic Park in Maplewood, New Jersey, the fabulous carrousel, above and left, is the oldest Magic Kingdom® attraction. Disney refurbished the ornate structure's 72 horses (no two are exactly alike) and hand-painted the wooden canopy with scenes from *Cinderella*. The carrousel was renovated again in 1987. Skyway to Tomorrowland, right, gives guests a one-way lift with a spectacular birds-eye view of both Fantasyland and Tomorrowland.

Cinderella Castle

This storybook castle, inspired by elaborate European castles of the 12th and 13th centuries, is the symbol of a world where fantasy transcends reality. Inside, five intricate murals—created with millions of bits of Italian glass in more than 500 different colors, plus real silver and 14-karat gold—tell the timeless story of Cinderella and her prince, inset.

1971

Dumbo the Flying Elephant

Mad Tea Party

It's up, up, and away with Dumbo, above, one of the most popular Magic Kingdom® rides. New Dumbo ride vehicles were added in 1993. Left, pastel-colored teacups, out of a scene from *Alice in Wonderland*, spin wildly in the Mad Tea Party.

MICKEY MOUSE REVUE

A cast of lovable Disney characters performed in this musical attraction until 1980, with the orchestra led by Maestro Mickey himself, below. The attraction moved to Tokyo Disneyland, and its Magic Kingdom® home became the Fantasyland Theater, today housing Legend of the Lion King.

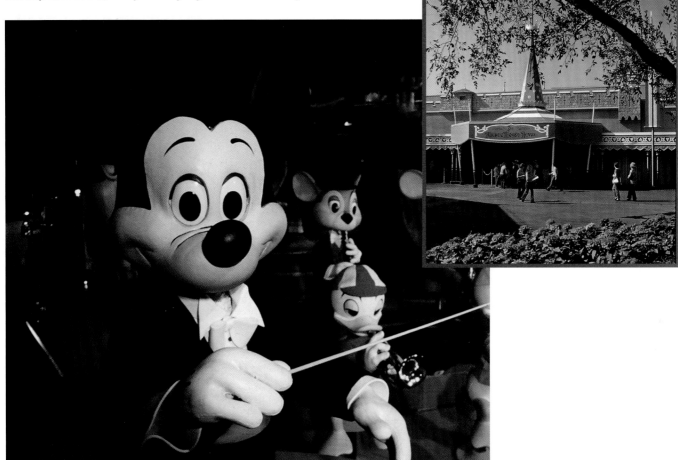

1971

PETER PAN'S FLIGHT

Tinker Bell leads the way as guests soar over the rooftops in Captain Hook's ship to Never Land in this enchanting attraction, inspired by Scottish writer Sir James M. Barrie's play about the boy who wouldn't grow up.

SNOW WHITE'S SCARY ADVENTURE

Guests sense that they're riding though the original Walt Disney movie classic in this attraction, now called Snow White's Adventures after its revision in 1995.

Mr. Toad's Wild Ride

This lighthearted attraction takes guests along with Mr. J. Thaddeus Toad, left, as he zigs and zags along the road to Nowhere in Particular in scenes from the classic novel *The Wind in the Willows*. Above, some of the silly chaos along the way.

Did You Know?

Since 1971, more than 8 million "mouse ear" hats have been purchased by Walt Disney World® Resort guests. The familiar black ears became a definitive fad when the Mouseketeers wore them on the *Mickey Mouse Club*, which began airing on ABC in October 1955, and the hats were sold by mail order for 69 cents.

IT'S A SMALL WORLD

The definitive, old-
fashioned Disney
attraction It's a Small
World first opened at
the New York World's
Fair in 1964-65, and its
theme song is one of
the best-known Disney
tunes of all time.
Guests board boats for
a fanciful trip through
enchanted foreign
lands populated with
hundreds of Audio-
Animatronic dolls.

20,000 Leagues Under the Sea

This underwater attraction in the beautiful Fantasyland lagoon took guests on an imaginative journey with Captain Nemo, past giant fish, clams, sea horses, and even the lost city of Atlantis. There also was an attack by the legendary giant squid, right, that Jules Verne described in his classic novel. The seaworthy vessels were built in Tampa, Florida, then trucked to the Magic Kingdom® Park, top right. The attraction closed in 1994.

1971

TOMORROWLAND

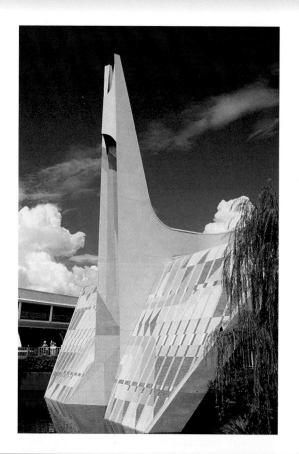

Disney's early vision of the future was an austere city with gleaming white towers, rocket ships ready for blast-off, and an innovative people mover. Now that vision has been updated to a Buck Rogers–like neighborhood like those imagined by sci-fi writers and moviemakers of the 1920s and 1930s. But for many, there's a wistful nostalgia connected to the original Tomorrowland, debuting at a time when mankind's opportunities in space seemed limitless.

GRAND PRIX RACEWAY

FLIGHT TO THE MOON

Grand Prix Raceway, now Tomorrowland Speedway, is a thrill for youngsters eager to hop behind the wheel of a race car. Flight to the Moon (later Mission to Mars until it closed in 1992 to make way for The ExtraTERRORestrial Alien Encounter), top right and right, simulated a flight into outer space. America the Beautiful (later American Journeys, until it closed in 1994 to make way for The Timekeeper) took guests on a Circle-Vision 360 trek across the United States, below.

AMERICA THE BEAUTIFUL

ELECTRICAL WATER PAGEANT

One of longest-running shows at the Walt Disney World® Resort, the Electrical Water Pageant lights up Bay Lake and the Seven Seas Lagoon every night of the year, weather permitting. Top photo shows the spectacular special edition for the Fourth of July. The sparkling pageant is a string of floating structures covered with tiny lights to represent whimsical creatures.

FANTASY IN THE SKY FIREWORKS

This incomparable show first blazed in the nighttime sky above Cinderella Castle in 1971, choreographed to music with amazing perfection. And when Tinker Bell flies in the finale with the castle all aglow, children of all ages really du believe in magic.

1971

BE OUR GUEST

DISNEY'S CONTEMPORARY RESORT

This giant A-frame structure was the first Walt Disney World® Resort hotel, designed with room for the monorail to run through its massive lobby, above. Impressive, 90-foot-high mosaic murals of Native American children, top right, decorate the concourse.

DISNEY'S POLYNESIAN RESORT

Lush tropical gardens, traditional longhouses, and a white-sand beach create a breath-taking South Seas ambience on the shores of the Seven Seas Lagoon.

1971

Disney's Fort Wilderness Resort & Campground

Set in nearly 800 acres of pines and cypress, this relaxed resort offers a nightly campfire with movies and cartoons, left; fishing in the canals, bottom left; and canoeing, bottom right—just a few of the myriad outdoor activities. Chip 'n' Dale, below, are the official mascots of the campground.

DISNEY'S DINNER SHOWS

Dinner shows, past and present, have provided Walt Disney World® Resort guests with many fun-filled hours. In 1971 the Polynesian Revue, left, premiered at Disney's Polynesian Resort. The Hoop-Dee-Doo Musical Revue, above, at Disney's Fort Wilderness Resort & Campground opened in 1974 and is still going strong. From 1981 to 1993, Broadway at the Top, above left, featured talented singers and dancers performing Broadway hits in Disney's Contemporary Resort's Top of the World restaurant. At every holiday season since 1992, Goofy plays Santa Claus in the Jolly Holiday show in Disney's Contemporary Resort Convention Center.

1971